# Aperture

# Aperture

## by Blaine Marchand

BuschekBooks

Ottawa

*For Kant:*
*Thanks for all you have done for making the Poe Train happen. I look forward to reading your work. Until next we meet,*
*blaine*

*Poe Train*
*Ottawa to Vancouver*
*April 16-27, 2015*

Text and photographs copyright © 2008 Blaine Marchand
*All rights reserved.*

Library and Archives Canada Cataloguing in Publication

Marchand, Blaine, 1949-
    Aperture / by Blaine Marchand.

Poems.
ISBN 978-1-894543-46-0

    1. Afghanistan--Poetry. 2. Afghanistan--Pictorial works.
3. Marchand, Blaine, 1949- --Travel--Afghanistan. I. Title.

PS8576.A633A76 2008      C811'.54      C2008-903622-0

Printed in Winnipeg, Manitoba, by Hignell Book Printing.

BuschekBooks
P.O. Box 74053
5 Beechwood Avenue
Ottawa, Ontario K1M 2H9
Canada

BuschekBooks gratefully acknowledges the support of the Canada Council for the Arts for its publishing program.

*This book is dedicated to the unnamed poet who read his poem in the Shalmanar refugee camp. His poem introduced me to the fierce pride and the determination of the Afghan people to rebuild amidst the destruction of their country.*

*It is also dedicated to Filippo Grandi and the people of UNHCR who worked so diligently to help the Afghan refugees retain their human dignity and return to their homeland.*

Contents

| | |
|---|---|
| Prologue | viii |
| Disheartened Afghans | 2 |
| 1. Leave-taking | 5 |
| Panorama | 8 |
| 2. Into the North West Frontier Province, Pakistan | 9 |
| This Enclosure | 14 |
| 3. The Home Coming | 16 |
| Kabul | 20 |
| 4. On the Way to Kabul | 22 |
| In the British Cemetery | 26 |
| 5. Kabul | 28 |
| Inching Forward | 32 |
| 6. Flying to Kandahar | 34 |
| Equilibrium | 36 |
| 7. Kandahar | 38 |
| Refuge | 42 |
| 8. Leave Taking | 43 |
| Renegade | 46 |
| *Apis dorsata* | 47 |
| Barter | 50 |
| The Pull of Gravity | 54 |
| Marking Time | 55 |
| Relinquishing the Spell | 58 |
| Maestro | 62 |
| As It Once Was | 63 |
| Apparition | 66 |
| Zakat | 67 |
| Fragment | 70 |
| Dust | 71 |

List of Illustrations

| | |
|---|---|
| Cover | Day Break, Herat |
| 6 | On the Way to School, Herat |
| 7 | In the British Cemetery, Kabul |
| 12 | About to Depart, Peshawar, Pakistan |
| 13 | Learning a Trade, Shalmanar Refugee Camp, Pakistan |
| 18 | Shoes, Shalmanar Boys School, Pakistan |
| 19 | Jirga, Shalmanar Refugee Camp, Pakistan |
| 24 | Hindu Kush, Kabul |
| 25 | The Palace from Camp Julien, Kabul |
| 30 | Khyber Pass Valley |
| 31 | Khyber Pass Border Inspection |
| 34 | General Massoud, Shomali Plains |
| 35 | Vendors on Chicken Street, Kabul |
| 40 | Kabul River |
| 41 | Red Flags, Afghanistan |
| 44 | Girl in a Silver Dress, Kabul |
| 45 | In the British Cemetery, Kabul |
| 48 | Mugging for the Camera, Blue Mosque, Mazar-e Sharif |
| 49 | Preparing for Tomorrow, Shalmanar Girls' School, Pakistan |
| 52 | The Conversation, Blue Mosque, Mazar-e Sharif |
| 53 | Three Women Walking, Kabul |
| 56 | Corona Bike, Kabul |
| 57 | Waiting, Peshawar, Pakistan |
| 60 | Devotees, Blue Mosque Mazar-e Sharif |
| 61 | Sweepers, Blue Mosque, Mazar-e Sharif |
| 64 | Grandmother and Child, Kabul |
| 65 | Arriving Home, Jalalabad |
| 68 | Pine Tree, Jalalabad |
| 69 | Crossing the Border, Khyber Pass |
| 73 | Boy with Kite, Kabul |
| 74 | Devotee, Blue Mosque, Mazar-e Sharif |
| 75 | Women in White, Blue Mosque, Mazar-e Sharif |
| 76 | In the British Cemetery, Kabul |
| 77 | Newspaper Boys, Chicken Street, Kabul |
| 78 | Dove Seller, Blue Mosque, Mazar-e Sharif |

Prologue

One experiences a new country in different ways—filtered through the mind, instantaneously through the senses and finally through memories. Together these form a triptych which can be read in the context of their individual scene or as a panorama. Most commonly, a triptych is a painting or carving which has three panels. It also can be three musical compositions which are linked by a common theme and usually composed by one person. But, at one time, a triptych was three bound writing tablets.

My first exposure to Afghanistan was in October of 2003 when I was part of an eight donor-country mission to Pakistan, Afghanistan and Iran. The delegates met with Afghan refugees-in-exile in Pakistan and Iran, as well as with returned refugees in Afghanistan. Encountering these disenfranchised people was my first introduction to their fierce pride and determination to rebuild their lives despite the devastation of their homeland.

Men and women (when I was allowed to meet with women) spoke most frequently of their fundamental desire for security, stability and peace in their birthplace. They were worn out from living under the lawlessness of the gun. Paramount was their longing to make a living so their children could grow stronger, could prosper.

More often than not, I sat in jirga (council) meetings and listened to a language I could not understand. But I could grasp their plight in the despondent rhythms of their voices. Through an interpreter, I was permitted a glimpse into their struggles during the oppression of the Communist and Taliban regimes, of their harrowing flights from a war that wrecked havoc on villages and homes, on innocent bystanders. And land they had formerly owned was now in the hands of others.

In this initial mission, I kept a notebook of my daily meetings and took occasional photographs. These were impressions that struck me as I witnessed the overwhelming poverty in refugee camps in Pakistan, the turmoil of migrant workers in Iran who faced deportation. By contrast, there was the simple dignity of the Afghans who had returned to repossess their homes and their lives. Afghans, I discovered, are an entrepreneurial, industrious people.

The juxtaposition of widespread destruction in Afghanistan and the creativity of Afghans was startling. The beauty of the stark landscape and the chaos of life in Kabul and Kandahar were unsettling. The movement of people going about their daily lives while helicopters churned overhead was disquieting. Afghanistan was a mysterious land which drove roots into my senses.

Over the next two years, I visited Afghanistan four times, traveling to Kabul, Jalalabad, Kandahar, Herat and Mazur-e-sharif, among other sites. Again and again, the people and the scenes forged their way into my imagination. They left an indelible mark.

Since 1995 and the publication of my fifth book of poetry, *Bodily Presence*, I had withdrawn from writing poetry. I no longer believed I could write. Perhaps, I rationalized to myself, I had simply written myself out. Poetry I told myself, trying to justify the silence, no longer mattered. It did not reach out to people. Yet, everywhere I went in Afghanistan, people quoted poetry when they spoke. Poetry is integral to how they interpret the world. The words of their esteemed poets, committed to memory, give Afghanistan, a land of many peoples, a common voice, and a reference point. Quotations are heard in politicians' speeches, in the day-to-day banter of shop keepers, in the greetings refugees offer to visitors.

On one of my visits, lying awake, all of the images I had absorbed and the resonance in the rhythms of people's speech, led to an outpouring of poetry that I immediately wrote down. I continued to do this on subsequent visits and did so as I worked on this manuscript. The Afghan people had rekindled and given me back my poetic voice. They showed me the way out of the self-imposed exile in which I had displaced myself.

One of the constant themes within my poetic work has been the experience of traveling in developing countries. A foreign country makes you question your perceptions of the world. It makes you see more clearly how Canada shapes your view of the world. And it makes you question the assumptions you make about people and other countries.

To me, a country is its people. This triptych captures the Afghans I met and observed. I cannot claim it speaks for them, but these poems are an offering of gratitude to them for returning me to the creative form I love deeply.

*Disheartened Afghans*

*with their war-torn lives,*
*belong to nowhere, except*
*to the heart of the dark mountains.*
*Look carefully into our faces,*
*do you see anything there,*
*except pure misery?*

*Do not look down on us,*
*although miserable.*
*There are no other refugees*
*more lonely, more harmless*
*or more miserable than we are.*

*Dead we are. But we still*
*stare back at life.*
*I am telling you this*
*because I want you*
*to understand.*
*I am telling you this*
*because I do not want you*
*to let go*
*of my hand.*

*Widows and unhappy orphans*
*live contained in the boundaries*
*of this camp. Believe me,*
*no one cares. No security*
*in the country, no money*
*in our pockets. The situation*
*gets tighter all the time.*
*It tightens and tightens like a chain.*

*Yes, you, our great guest
and honourable elder, do not
let go of my hand, do not
leave me in this place.*

*Where should I go?
What is my destiny?
I am just another refugee
among many refugees.
By title, a merchant. But here
I know not what I am.
My only hope is with you.*

*The past happened
without you. My time is over.
But now that you have come,
do not dishearten us.*

(poem read during a jirga by a poet in Shalmanar refugee camp)

1.     Leave-taking

Tomorrow I leave for Afghanistan, a country I know largely from the ghostly television images of night-vision military manoeuvres in the war against terror. This afternoon, I am thinking back to the late 1970s when I went with a friend to an astrologer. In drawing up my chart, he predicted I would go overseas. Though he could not tell when it would be, he added that I would never return. Could this voyage be destiny playing its final hand?

Initially I was vaguely aware, at a sub-conscious level, that there might be danger. So many friends voiced concern that gradually their skittishness filtered into me. Yet this is an opportunity that excites me—the chance to see, firsthand, the plight of refugees and the struggle of those who have chosen to return to their destroyed homeland. I will experience through my own eyes a land and a people I know only through cut-and-paste texts I prepare as briefing notes that keep me at the office all hours.

I am on a bus on the first part of the passage into the heart of the Silk Road. It is a cool, brilliant autumn day. The fields along the highway are russet and chrome yellow, bordered by maples beginning their vibrant pageantry. The sun, lying low in the western sky, casts long shadows that fall easterly across the land—the direction of this journey toward the unknown.

Panorama

The ridges of mountains
and deserts, remnants of snow
are wisps of thinning hairs along
the folds of elders' hands
as they sit cross-legged,
holding counsel.

Clouds trace patterns
along the hills' arms,
tattoos inscribed over muscle—
though deep within valleys
along meandering veins of river
are luxuriant fields
coaxed by broad hands,
emaciated by warfare
and deprivation. The desert
brought into bearing
despite years of drought and depletion,

remains stoic as generations
come and go, successive
invasions scarring with building
and destroying, waves of migration,
seasonal birds fleeing
and then returning when the weather
quickens with response.

This land, the colour of dried blood,
can be viewed simply as panorama.
Or as metaphor, geography
carving history—
a sculptor engraving script
into hard, mute stone;
a poet pleading, scribing
the voices of people onto pages
fine and dry as the sand the wind
plucks, sowing the air with nettles.

## 2. Into the North West Frontier Province, Pakistan

This highway takes us deeper into the region that borders Afghanistan. Such a desolate landscape, it is nothing but sparse vegetation, a scrawny tree or shrub bristling from the earth, struggling to survive. Goats munch on whatever clump of greenery they can find. They precariously balance perpendicular on dirt ridges or on a branch as their pink tongues tug at vines that grow over stubby trees, among rocks or within the bristles of cacti. Their front lips gingerly draw the vegetation into their mouths.

We turn off the main road; head down a narrow passage into a village where the compounds are so close you could reach through the window and touch the sun-baked mud walls. Heavy metal doors, inset with spade-like designs, are shut tight, bolted. What lies on the other side? We round a corner and a door lies open a crack. Children play in a barren courtyard. It is but a fleeting glimpse.

Before, this was a refugee camp—a sea of tents holding 60,000 people. In 2002, people started to return to Afghanistan. There are only about 28,000 refugees left. The remaining buildings are tumble-down, their jagged edges like broken teeth. Some are occupied but officials prefer to pull down the remnants rather than have them become hiding places for bandits or the Taliban.

We drive up to a medical centre. Against white-washed walls are clutches of women in thrown back blue burqas, girls in tangerine and persimmon and boys in mocha and charcoal. All stand waiting. Most of the children have rust coloured hair, a sign of malnutrition. TB is rampant. The women draw down the burqas to hide their faces as we approach.

As we leave clinic, there is a green mesh, under which an herb garden is lush, aromatic to my touch. Yarrow, tansy and basil weave a mirage of scent amid such aridness.

We go to visit a girls' school. Row upon row of plastic shoes loll about, abandoned in the corridor. Inside the classroom, girls recite their lessons. At the front, a girl with a stick points to a script floating across a page taped to the wall. She enunciates each word carefully which the class repeats back to her. The girls bob back and forth like small boats on water as they repeat each word. We start to leave but are asked to wait. Eight girls stand and sing the Afghan national anthem.

Next, we stop where the boys learn. Four classrooms and a tent outside for the older boys. In one room, they are doing sums by making calculations with their fingers. There are no books. The teacher invites a boy up to demonstrate the technique. The boy's eyes are full of mischief. It is a chance to show off, a display of bravado.

Then we drop into a vocational centre for the disabled, veterans of the war. Men work in open-air rooms—at shoe-making, metal-working, masonry. After their lessons, they cross the yard to learn to read and do elementary math. Beyond, a room is sheathed by a cloth door. An Iranian-Canadian woman says that here the men's wives and daughters are taught embroidery, clothes making and carpet weaving. I lift the fabric to go in but as the women pull their scarves over their faces I mumble an apology and step back into the courtyard.

In a community centre, we meet elders who sit cross-legged on carpets. With their mushroom caps, their work-worn faces and their beards, they seem like elves. They greet us warmly; then, through interpreters, enumerate their concerns, the difficulties they and their families face. They want lives free of fighting and destruction. They long to return to the villages they fled due to the war.

We proceed to where iris scans are done. Irises are as distinctive as the whorls of fingerprints. A crippled man with a crutch hobbles over with three small children in tow. All are wearing black ragged clothes that hang down like damp ribbons. He shouts, shakes his crutch in the air. Workers step forward, calm him. He and the children slump to the ground.

We are on to the next site. The roadway we are on has crumbled away at the edges. Ruts are so large the vehicle must creep forward. We rock back and forth in our seats whenever a tire sinks and slides off course. Beyond is a graveyard—raised tombs of embedded stones, chunks of shale propped upright are markers. Rail-thin poles curve with the wind that yanks crimson strips of cloth with such force. We descend into a dry riverbed, slip over up a small incline, and pass through gates. Do these gates protect those within or keep others out?

A chairman greets us warmly and leads us into a tent. A small thin man, he assumes his appointed place behind a desk. On either side of him, in water glasses, are purple froths of basil. A marble pen and pencil set rests on a red and black carpet, one side of which is unraveling but secured to the table by nails. His speech is a mixture of pride and self-importance. He responds to our questions in long complicated phrases. An assistant politely jumps in, rendering his meandering replies into short phrases we easily understand.

Next, our group is divided into men and women. The men meet with another group of elders. Two interpreters, who have been selected, compete with each other to translate the refugees' needs. At one point, one man, exasperated by our questions, reprimands us: they may be displaced but they know what is happening on either side of the border through contacts and family networks. A poet, famous in this camp, reads one of his works. He holds his paper tightly, but it still quakes in his hands. He recites the poem from memory. I understand nothing, but the rhythm of the words, the catch in his voice, hints at its meaning.

As we begin the steep ascent up a hillside, it begins to rain heavily. Through the mist lies the Khyber Rifles fort. The vehicle twists and turns up the switchback road. The sky clears. We descend from our vehicle and are led to an amphitheatre where we take our places and gaze out at the magnificent gorge that is the valley of the Khyber Pass. There is a frisson of excitement at being in such a fabled place. In front of us is a large papier mache mock-up of the valley complete with coloured lights, mock towers and tiny blue signs with carefully printed names on them. A ramrod soldier stands at a podium and begins a lecture on the history of the Pass. The microphone cuts on and off, distorts his speech. His pointer jumps from place to place as he explains the waves of migration that passed this way, the colonial struggle to take control of the Valley. As his pointer hovers above each mock tower, the coloured light next to it blinks off and on. To his left, a young soldier, serious with intent, flips chart paper. On each one, the name is carefully printed in red block letters. A Khyber Pass power point.

This Enclosure

The flamboyant roses—
orange inferno, oxidized red,
incandescent yellow—transform
this courtyard to a retreat,
a dream keeping distant
the din and danger of the world.

As darkness clamps down,
a helicopter hovers, its propeller
frantic, a terrified heart,
and then a low whistle, a pitch
of breath through puckered mouth.

Lying jet lagged, drifting
in an out, hours of travel sifting
through my veins,
sand through torque of an hourglass,
I wonder momentarily
have I dreamt this?
My imagination held hostage
by warnings from well-intentioned friends.

Earlier, as the armoured vehicle
trundled down the deeply rutted street,
splotches of repaint along its side
—bullet holes or simple repairs?—
we waded through
clusters of schoolgirls,
long black coats, white scarves
feather their heads,
spilling over their shoulders.
The girls caught up
in the enthusiastic banter,
excitement and hope,
their future notepads
waiting for inscription.

One girl's scarf had slipped off,
avian, hovering in the wind, a wing.
Her fine brown hair was taken up,
repeated in the ridges of foothills
behind her, sentinels
that hover about this city.


When I wandered to my room for rest
the roses, just watered,
intoxicated the air,
vital as the schoolgirls' clamour
which still loiters over the rutted road,
while their small hands reiterate,
tremble the steel door of this enclosure,
as if ephemera. Petals.

3.  The Home Coming

Refugees cross here from Pakistan, arriving in day-glow painted buses crammed well beyond capacity with families. Behind them follow lines of jingle trucks, so called due to metal bangles, suspended from chains, that clang against each other. These vehicles are piled high and wide, higgledy-piggledy in all directions with string beds, lumber and branches, all held together by a cat's cradle of rope tied to the front and back bumpers. The refugees disembark and proceed to a sheltered area where their identity books are checked. They enter a health clinic and then proceed to a legal aid centre for further referral. They leave and walk to a large tent where a demonstration about the dangers of landmines is given. Shells, mortars and devices are laid out on table cloths imprinted with these instruments of death.

Children huddle in front of a television. A cartoon explains the dangers. They are taught that stones painted red signal danger. White ones say walk close to these, this area is safe. Notepads and pencils are distributed so the children can write down or draw their thoughts. How do they absorb the cruel infliction left behind by their country's invaders?

Finally, heads of families receive their resettlement money, based on the number of family members and the distance they have traveled. A man runs forward, shouts loudly that last year the rate for returnees was higher. The officials here are suspicious; quickly discuss among themselves whether he had been through before and has come back this year to get more money or whether a relative had told him the amount given last year. They quickly surround him, calmly explain things to him.

A headman welcomes us to his village, which has been selected for us to visit. He is tall and thin, with a grizzled white beard. A grey and black turban is tied to one side in a flourish of knot that sits against his head like an exotic moth, a pinstripe of ash edging its wings. Gold-framed glasses magnify his eyes; the way autumn dust distorts the moon, making it appear lopsided. His broad hand gestures, his stance suggests someone born to this position, proud of this rebuilt village.

We walk down winding paths to a compound and pass through a gate pushed open. At last, I am beyond the high mud walls. To the right is a latrine; to the left, close to the house, a bake oven. A slim sapling swerves up from the earth. Its bark indicates it is an apple tree. A sapphire wooden door is ajar. Its vibrant colour is startling. Beyond, three rooms house seven children, four girls and three boys ranging in age from 13 to one year. The eldest girl, who wears a rose tunic over pants, has a gold and brown head scarf with crimson flowers on it. It flows down from her head and is casually strewn over one shoulder. She is handicapped. Her mother, who huddles on a carpet in a dark corner of one room, is shrouded in a patterned cloth. Her father's eyes are wary and his face lined beyond his age.

Next, the headman takes us to a hand pump the community has recently installed. Men and boys circle the site. They stand with their arms folded and wear white turbans and caps. Every boy in the front row is shoed in white plastic sandals. The headman beckons to a young boy in an avocado shalwar kameez who leaps forward and frantically pumps the handle. Water spills over the concrete base and onto the ground. Other boys break rank, push forward but guards with rifles motion them back. At a distance, five young girls wearing shades of jade, vermillion and black wait patiently with empty pails.

We visit an irrigation canal that allows the people to coax cash crops from the arid ground, provides clean drinking water, and powers a turbine for a mill. The canal's edge is lush with grass, shrubs and trees. Women and girls squat on large rocks stained by the damp kaleidoscope of clothes they have washed. The girls stand up as we pass. I turn and look back. They silently watch us go up the stairs that rise beside the cascading flow that tumbles down to where they are clustered.

We head out and drive into Jalalabad, once the winter capital for the Afghan royal family. It is raining dust in our wake. Women in burqas pull the cloth that falls down from the shuttlecock crowns; shake it, and the grime from the lace work shifts onto their clothes beneath.

We visit a vocational school for women. All had fled to Pakistan during the worst of the war, stayed there for years but decided two years ago they had to return. Five are widows while the others head their families as all traces of their husbands have been lost. They dream of setting up a cooperative so they can feed and educate their children.

Through a domed gate we enter the residence of the governor of Jalalabad. It is a secret garden where everything is lush. Hedges and expanses of lawn flank both sides of the driveway. We disembark from the land rover to be greeted by a long line of men. We go into an ornate building, along a spacious corridor and into a formal room whose centerpiece is a massive carmine carpet. Sofas line the edges of the room, flanking an ornate chair that has the air of a throne. We expectantly wait the governor's arrival.

Kabul

is enclosures—
beyond the broken roads,
the tumult of cars and people,
away from the dust
that drapes everything,
high walls and metal doors
cloister profuse gardens
where sandy loam breaks open,
hoists vigorous stocks and shrubs
bowed down with saffron and scarlet.

is camouflage—
on corners, in front of residences
soldiers in uniforms
discoloured as the desert
brandish weapons
while along narrow, archaic streets
built for wooden wheel and hoof,
rumble tanks, heavy belts girding
the grinding wheels that churn up
compacted earth in drifts of dust.

is cleft—
after years of waged war,
buildings are flimsy, twisted
metal and concrete, compound fractures
dangling precarious
in the wind. They are phantoms
to be guessed at
whether specters of sinister occupation or
pomp and circumstance of palatial history.

is influx—
people returned after fighting,
metal shops laden with
marbled carcasses of butchered meat,

potted plants heavy with plump oranges
or a flurry of flowers. At corners, slapdash
lean-tos cater to immediate need,
be it retorquing an out-of-kilter wheel
or the repair of a down-at-the-heel shoe
by adolescents, thin and ratty,
always at the ready to shine it
back to lustre.

is the maimed—
widows, draped in burqas
faded to a milky blue,
wander into traffic, desperate,
tap at windows for a ragged Afghani
to buy food, nourish their children.
Grown men and young boys, sticks under arms
propped into a semblance of stance,
idle aimlessly on streets,
pant legs flapping flags, phantom limbs
reminders of what once was,
those released by death.

## 4. On the Way to Kabul

This morning, at breakfast, there were rumours that there was a coup in Kabul last night. Uncertainty and dread were palpable as we ate our meal in stunned silence. En route, through the raspy security radio system, we learn it did not take place. We are to continue on.

The hills and mountains are sentinels, denuded of trees. The Kabul River meanders at a short distance away. Sporadically along its sandy banks are the windblown tents of the Kouchies, nomadic people. Women and girls wear clothes of crimson, orange and purple. They are slashes of colour moving against the muted surroundings of their backdrop. Camels crouch beside tents, oblivious to everything around them, content to chew their cuds. At a distance, men and boys herd shaggy goats, which have blotches of blue and pink on their coats. In the foreground, remnants of tanks litter the roadside. Pathways of white or red rocks mark mine fields.

The road worsens as we weave our way through a series of narrow gullies. High walls of boulders perch precariously along their edges. One has plummeted and lodged in the roadway, blocking it. The vehicle manoeuvres around it. The river at some points is a mere trickle; at others, a torrent. The water is brown, although at one point it turns a deep blue.

We come to a halt. In front of us lies a jam of cars and yellow and white taxis. (Two hours, customers are promised, Jalalabad to Kabul.) A truck ahead is laden down with a lopsided burden of white sacks held in place by large tires secured by a web of rope. An overnight torrential downpour has turned the road into sludge. Traffic is blocked by an overloaded truck which slants precariously into the steep incline, its cab stopped by a wall of mud. Men gather on all sides, assess the situation, chat. Dressed in white, all are pristine. How do they do it?

The guards, who have been accompanying us, jump off their trucks, circle our land rover. Their guns are a menace in their hands as they steer people away, bystanders merely curious at a vehicle filled with foreigners.

The guards begin to shout, badger other drivers to pull over and allow us to pass through. An argument erupts beside our vehicle. Two guards push a screaming man, back him up against a low crumbling wall that barely separates the roadway from the gully below.

After endless discussion and debate, a pass-through is made. Oncoming vehicles slip by us spattering mud and water across our land rover. When it is the turn of vehicles heading to Kabul, the guards attempt to stem the flow so we can go first. But a rush of cars and taxis defeats their efforts, fills the breach with spinning wheels as drivers try to navigate out of the ruts. Finally each vehicle inches forward and we are on our way.

In the British Cemetery

The large door is weather-beaten,
black paint blistered, wood wormholed.
Its coarse thickness shuts out the daily din,
persistent grind of motors—cars, trucks
and bikes that clog the street, the heat
of their wheels pluming the air
with ash. Hidden inside,
a chaotic ramble, bone-thin trees,
wild grass and weeds, though
here and there flowers struggle
to retain some fragment of bloom.
They are flashpoints, memories
overtaken and trapped.

Propped up at irregular angles,
weights of stone lurch
as if forever uncomfortable
in their place of rest.
Here, a French woman
gunned down as she returned
from working with refugees.
Photo, a blur of blue veil,
cameos a face forever young,
gaze direct, innocent,
challenging your presence here.
Her vault, as if buried in France,
arrayed with crumbling bouquets.
Beside it, an elderly Jesuit's
stalwart white rock, high
on a rise, upright
as his faith, on which words
etched and highlighted
annotate a life given over
to conversion, the gospel of Jesus.
Beyond, in the back mud wall,
granite, durable as the Canadian

Shield, a black maple leaf,
a list, names and dates,
three soldiers reported
as collateral damage.

How long before these,
like the other tumbledown markers
littering this ground,
are muted, ravaged
by time, lost to memory?
A foreigner wandering
aimlessly, trying to decipher
the names, second-guess
at the stories, caught
inside these walls, in the shift
of time, removed from
the scurry of people and vehicles.

5.     Kabul

In the slow descent into Kabul, the air and the earth blend, seem smudged. On the outskirts, we pass through an industrial area, past the ISAF camp and the airport littered with skeletons of planes. The heart of the city is vibrant with people milling about its streets. Crowded shops are stacked high with blush apples, green melons, and red pomegranates. Behind the stalls, buildings collapse in on themselves. Those still standing are riddled with bullet holes.

Every now and again, an armed vehicle rumbles down the roadway, the steel treads girdling the wheels churn up the roadway. A soldier, perched in a turret in the centre, scans the horizon as the turret slowly rotates. Its armored belly, a modern-day Trojan horse, conceals officers whose inward arms nestle rifles. A flag flaps from an aerial that curves and is secured to the back of the steed. Many are red and white; in the centre a maple leaf.

The streets are clotted with traffic. Cars, trucks, land rovers, taxis and donkey carts all battle for their place on the roadway. The revving engines are reminiscent of verbal confrontation as the drivers inch their way through intersections and down narrow streets as if passing through the eye of a needle. Bikes, more often than not with a passenger astride a back carrier, weave in and out of vehicles, literally cheek by jowl. How do the bike riders and drivers keep their equilibrium when the roadways are so precarious, full of ruts some of which crumble away into the gutter beside them? It is 1 p.m. Government offices have closed and men are making their way to prayer.

We are to meet an Afghan Minister. The cityscape blurs as we turn left and right, round this corner and that. I am disoriented. Are we always passing the same roundabout, buildings with that bland utilitarian Soviet architectural style? They are supposedly models of efficiency, yet frequently lack the critical amenities—water, heat and electricity.

Down the side of one building hangs a gigantic portrait of General Ahmed Shah Massoud, the Mujahideen leader who was assassinated two days before 9-11. (Mujahideen, our interpreter tells us, means struggler in Arabic.) Some people speculate that the timing of his death and the attack in New York were linked.

We turn down a wide street chock-a-block with official buildings. On the top of their high walls corkscrews of barbwire unravel. In front of each building is a guard hut and firmly padlocked gates. Uniformed men clutch rifles aggressively, ready to make the first move. Along the roadway are trees, like sentinels, with silver-grey and green trunks much like the camouflage fatigues of soldiers. The trees' leaves are yellow-brown. The hues of this city are autumnal.

Twilight is coming on. The traffic is stop and start. We halt at an intersection, wait for the light to change. Women in blanched burqas tap at the windows. A torn creased Afghani bill is held between fingers so we know the women's intent. They point at their open, toothless mouths. The vehicle jumps forward, turns right. A full-sized portrait of President Hamid Kharzi is lit up by floodlights. Nearby is the draped image of the martyred General Massoud—the old and new charismatic leaders of this country.

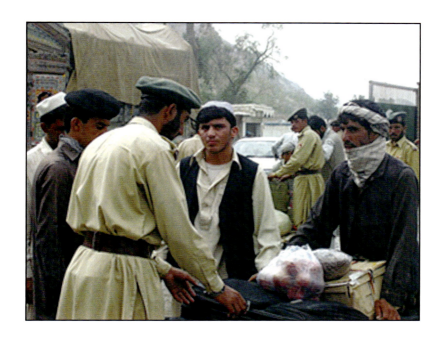

Inching Forward

A cubist painting—
four-wheel vehicles
navigating an intersection,
land rover chrome,
lemon yellow fenders of taxis,
tie-dyed trucks, tassels and bits of metal
swaying this way and that.
All inch forward,
mind over matter as brave drivers
with steel-eyed precision
coordinate turns of steering wheel
with feet on the gas pedal
all the while at the ready to brake.
The air aggressive
basso profundo of horns,
fists and voices pierced by anger.
In the middle, lost and struggling,
a lone policeman
whom nobody minds;
his signals and whistles
a whisper in the din and the revving.
Survival of the fittest;
only the dominant inch forward.

Yet amid this cacophony
men move so freely on bikes
darting in to any opening,
seizing the moment, advancing consistently.
They straddle their seats, upright and proud,
above and then beyond
this toil and labour of traffic.
One boy, tails of his white shirt
waving behind him in defiance
of the snarl, glides with ease
around the corner and down the street
of shattered homes and makeshift enterprise.

His bike, festooned,
a rainbow woven intricately

through the spikes that radiate
from the aluminum hub
of the wheels. Round and round,
red, orange, and yellow, unflagging,
blend in continuity.

6.     Flying to Kandahar

We climb into a small plane, buckle ourselves in. It taxis down the runway, its engines humming, its body vibrating as it gains speed. Lift off, we are airborne. The view through the window reveals that Kabul is larger, more spread out than is apparent from the ground. Everything is beige—earth, trees and residences in a monochromatic palette. The city is completely surrounded by mountains. Range after range, a deep purple colour, are spectacular. How can there be no discernible vegetation on all these mountains?

As we fly southward, there is little evidence of water though there are many channels gouged into the parched land. Miles and miles of unbroken sandy valleys lie between the mountain ranges. Now and again sunlight stitches silver into a river or a broach of lake.

At the beginning of this flight, the pilots had warned the descent into Kandahar would be steep. In the distance, a reddish line in the sand, where the desert soil turns ochre, runs as far as the eye can see. The plane tilts to a forty-five-degree angle. The plane's nose plunges toward the desert floor. Through the window, littered along the runway, is the wreckage of planes. Our bodies vibrate with the shell of the aircraft. We hold our breaths. A sudden leveling out, touch down. A collective audible sigh fills the cabin.

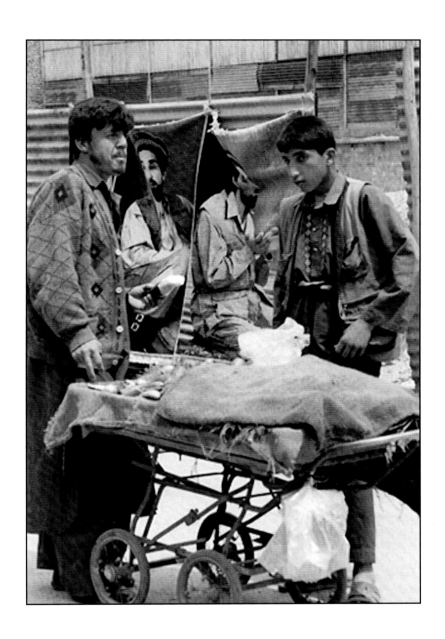

Equilibrium

How furious the man's legs pump
navigating so assiduously
at the precarious edge
of the ragged road,
swerving to the left,
then the right,
circumventing potholes,
ruts deep as ravines.
Pant cloth shivers in the wake
and the press of cars,
the blare of horns
unrelentingly staking claim
to their sovereign right to this street.
Amid all this, he maintains
equilibrium, his gaze fixed
forward, a study in concentration
never deviating, never for a moment
acknowledging the imminent danger,
the lurking potential for fatal crush
should his wheel plunge
or his foot slip from the pedal.

He cannot lose sight, for
on the back of his bike
perched astride the metal carrier
his wife, a queen on a barque
in portrait, hands tiny
against the stiff folds
of blue burqa flowing
from the tight cap of crown.
This over-garment, not permitting
common men to rest their eyes
upon her, or dust and diesel to stain
her skin though the hem of her covering,
caught up in a moment of motion,
has blown aside, revealing a dress

ornate with garlands of white lilies,
slim ankles crossed,
one sandal slipped from its binding
keeps its own beat in motion,
dangling dangerously, dancing.

7.     Kandahar

The road into town appears to be through a valley. In Kandahar, too, everything is in disrepair. But here, too, people go about their lives. They have set out their wares to sell in a long perpendicular square. At one side is a large archway that is being restored. Bamboo scaffolding surrounds it like bones picked clean.

Young men wear round flattop hats, called toppeyanay, which are embroidered and embedded with flowers, silver threads or mirrors that catch the light. At the forehead, the brim is cut away to form a vee through which one glimpses their dark hair. Many men ride bicycles with friends perched on the carrier on the back. It is a delicate balancing act to maintain equilibrium.

Older men, with long grey beards, wear concoctions of turban with a long cloth falling over their slender shoulders. Heavy woolen vests weigh down long shirts that billow around pants of the same colour and material.

We are on our way to meet the Governor of Kandahar, a former Minister in Kabul. As we enter his compound, a large building to the left is under construction. A large treed garden hems in the central walk. Border gardens are resplendent with grandiose roses. We go into a low white building and enter a conference room where we sit at a long table. The governor enters. He is about forty, has dark hair and a beard. His words come out slowly as he tells us about his province and the problems it faces in reintegrating of refugees, in particular the nomadic people. All this is so difficult for the Afghan Transitional Authority he says with a tinge of resignation in his voice.

We drive out of Kandahar along yet another roadway in disrepair. It is not just due to the ravages of war, but also the wear and tear of overloaded trucks that clog the route. Though everywhere there is destruction, elaborate homes are under construction.

"The people use imported brick rather than the traditional mud brick structures," our Afghan-Canadian interpreter tells us. "Where does their money come from?" He complains about the cost of land. Despite fourteen years in Canada, he still does not have enough money to buy land here.

He tells us he has brought his wife, but she must live in Quetta, Pakistan, where it is safer. Yet despite his words, he says he is optimistic though he warns that Afghans have tried Communism, then Talibanism, and now democracy. It must work.

I ask the interpreter if the landscape is green after winter when there is rain or moisture. He replies he has only been back in Afghanistan for a few months and this is not his region.

We drive for a long time, past a factory deliberately bombed out by the Russians just prior to their departure. Later, there is a blue and white mosaic mosque, its dome as if wrapped in sky.

We turn off the road. Gravel grumbles under the wheels, feathering the air with dust. Every once in a while, a truck full of Afghan soldiers veers to the side of the road in order to avoid the bumps, spilling its human load. The soldiers are rambunctious, whooping and hollering, scarves drawn across their faces to prevent the dust from entering their noses, mouths and ears.

We pull into a peanut and wool processing plant which generates income for Kouchies, who form the majority in the nearby resettlement. We are greeted by the Director and several dignitaries. We walk through a covered building where men sit cross-legged shelling peanuts. Their chatter echoes, reverberates against the concrete walls. The men fall silent when we enter. They watch us intently, their eyes following, taking in our every move. We pass into an attached shed where they are processing peanut oil and where the next buckets of peanuts wait to be shelled.

Outside they work on the wool. A man stands astride a mound of fleece, stomps on it with his feet while another man with a hose pours water over it. The director wants to tell us about the process but we are late and must hurry back to Kandahar. Being Friday, there are restrictions on flights into the Kabul airport.

We speed down the road as quickly as the gravel permits and then onto the highway, which is congested. The cars and trucks do not move aside despite the driver blaring the horn, as is the usual roadway procedure here. We are very late. He weaves in and out of traffic on both sides. A truck squeezes us to one side into the path of an oncoming vehicle which swerves toward the ditch to avoid us. A screech of brakes and it fishtails to a halt.

We arrive and drive straight onto the tarmac. We jump out of the vehicle, rush to the plane only to learn that the pilots have negotiated a new landing time. We have a few seconds to say goodbye to the interpreter and the driver. Courtesies count for much here.

The door of the plane is pulled tight. Propellers splice the air in continual motion. The engines rev up and the plane bolts down the runway. Take off. It circles, spiraling upward into the sky. The light fading from the sky imbues the landscape with an indigo haze. It is beautiful and haunting.

Refuge

It is only cloth. Blue, as the sky
once was above Kabul.
This garb, it girds women,
close as the shuttlecock
that snugly encases their heads.
The lattice looks through
the grill of a cloister. Its weight,
the burqa, a burden imposed.

Women make their way
through streets rampant with men
who gaze on butchered meat,
or who stand in groups tearing strips
of unleavened bread, their hairy fingers
thrust deep into ravenous mouths.
For these women, it is not
burdensome, its fabric
pleats, as if gauze, expand,
contract in the wind
as they walk. It is armour—
for nerves still cautious with memory,
and stories of mothers and aunts and sisters
marched into the sports stadium,
beaten and raped, their screams
rending the air with terror
which the men's ears translate
into frenzied cheers at soccer.

This weave is refuge,
a second layer
through which lascivious eyes
cannot peer. It is protection,
like walls around a house,
the shadow windswept pines
cast over the earth.
It is the expanse of sky
flowing up and over the Hindu Kush.

8.    Leave-taking

It is our last evening in Kabul so we ask if we can do a quick tour. We drive up and down streets through the approaching twilight. The hills are sown with pearls of light. Returnees have claimed this unused land to build homes. We enter an older part of Kabul, pass along the channel of the Kabul River, which is bone-dry due to a five-year drought that defeats the country. Collapsed buildings rub shoulders with ones being restored. Darkness gives the city a post-war gloom.

We drive past a building, a skeleton of its former self, high on a hill. We are uncertain what it is—a palace or a military headquarters? We take photos. It begins to snow, the flakes large and luxurious.

The flashes of our cameras draw three bedraggled children—a young boy in a lemon toque and a blue coat, a girl who has dark imprints on her cheeks (are they bruises?), the elder boy who wears only a sweat shirt despite the cold. He clutches a translucent plastic kite to his chest. They are curious. What are our good names? Where are we from? In return, we ask if we may take their photos, hand them freshly minted Afghanis in exchange. They take our money and run through the flurry into the night. The kite struggles up into the air behind them. The heavy snow distorts their figures as they disappear into the night. We have no idea where they came from or where they are going. They are fleeting metaphors of this country, ragged yet bright with spirit, hope.

Renegade

The wind is cruel, relentless,

an invasion come down from the mountains.
Conspiring with razor-edged rain
that shatters against and disfigures windows

as we drive by the remnants of the king's palace
which, like a skull hung out in a market square,
reprimands those who pass by.
Treason can still be dealt with by the sword.

The drizzle becomes turncoat, is snow clumping
in our disheveled clothes as we descend
to take photos of these remains
that bear witness to this land's precarious facade.

Three children, drawn by the silent explosion
of our electronic flashes, approach us.
Their ragtag clothes and frayed shoes
are soaked through. Rheum cakes their eyes.

Under and around the elder boy's arm,
a plastic square scuttles its tail
festooned with red strips.
He holds it securely, fearful it will be confiscated.

In the spring of each year, the sky
is a phalanx of tinted shapes in all sizes,
tethered to glass-coated strings, manipulated
in a skirmish to cut each other down.

Mindful that during the rule of enforced cruelty
this simple pleasure was forbidden, the boy,
although posing for our cameras, runs away.
Rising up, behind him, his kite

a renegade against the sky.

*Apis dorsata*

In this early evening, the moon is a husk,
a wasp's nest spun within the cupola
crowning the ruined palace. The waning sun
coats the stones of blasted windows
and pockmarked porticos in faux wax.
Wraithlike bands of gold permeate
their emptiness with an infusion, honeycomb.

Once this relic held promise, was an abode
of peace surrounded by gardens,
symbolized the dream of a king
for his people—their rights, their freedom.
When he fled, driven away, substance gone,
it was swarmed by successions of foragers,
giant bees congregating in a fallen tree.

Each cluster of scavengers, resolute
in their inclinations, performed a dance,
interpreted the bias of sun to sustenance,
and then pursued the polarized light.
The vibration of their wings in short bursts,
whether discourse of dogma or ravage of rifles,
was venomous, lethal as their stingers to intruders.

Barter

Remnants of Afghanistan rest
in this narrow dukan weighing down
the makeshift shelves of rough-hewn boards
piling high in the corners,
slumped,
a man drifts off to sleep.

Burgundy carpets, worn but decipherable
arabesque patterns on which elders once sat
with closed eyes, narrow fingers
scouring burnished beards
as villagers assembled for council.

Behind glass, chunks of stucco and chiseled stone
rubbed down to fine detail
have withstood time and disaster,
but not the skill, nor the greed,
of the plunderer's art.

Scenes from the Buddha's life: in meditation,
cross-legged on a lotus throne;
the fasting prophet, skin a flimsy fabric
stretched over his ribcage, that echoes
the folds of robe undulating over his emaciated arms.

There a flawless terracotta foot, serrated
above the ankle as if severed by a landmine;
while here is the vestige
of a face, a three-quarter moon against black cloth.

The merchant, a gnome of a man,
pads over spryly. His voice a chant
of recurring rhymes, its lightness
reminiscent of the sweet fluidity
of Kabul's spring air
that flows down from the Hindu Kush

and imbeds blossoms
among the struggling grasses in parched earth,
strews them over crumbling stones
that once were foundations.

Everywhere, ruins offset by remaking,
the struggle to survive.
Everything, human or object,
has a negotiable price.
Only his poem escapes:
words preset in antiquity, still vibrant
in his mouth.

.

The Pull of Gravity

The skin of the hand drum
taut, white, a full moon,
casts the singer's face in darkness.
All I can see is his wool vest
stitched in elaborate swirls,
an undecipherable calligraphy.
His long fingers scribe
the membrane, punctuate
his song in a language
unknown to me. I strain
to comprehend the nuances,
whether this lilt might praise
a lover's hair, his drop
in diction be the ache
for a childhood long past.

The audience under this canopy
is attentive to every gesture
as were the participants
a few months back
to each phrase offered
as they forged the future,
the Afghan constitution.

The singer's voice grows silent
but his thumb vibrates
the tambour, its pitch
an orator's diction
echoing through the air
in waves of repeating cadence
holding the listeners
drawing them in
by the pull of its gravity.

Marking Time

The boy swings back and forth,
a pendulum marking time,
his lungs, synchronized with air,
inaugurate an arc of song.
His hands grasp rough bark,
the limb of a pomegranate tree
barren as the land

behind him. Up a steep incline
shards of tilting rocks
mark the graves of Afghans
slaughtered over years
of discord. Here and there,
red cloth, worn by the veneration
of wind, oscillates from poles
bleached white as the bones
of martyrs ensconced

below. The boy's feet
against the fixed point of trunk
push him back into the space
that takes on the contour
of his sinuous body. To and fro,
to and fro, denoted by an innate rhythm
and instinctive delight in his voice,
he flies past the scarred landscape,
toward that opening, his future.

Relinquishing the Spell

Schoolboys drop their books,
lessons abandoned so they can skip along,
keep pace with this man swathed
in black—swirl of turban, backdrop of cape,
blouson of shirt and leggings.
His left hand holds
a whittled stick; his right
a long chain, tugged by a monkey
scampering in semi-circles
in a spangled pink dress

somersaults, turns herself
backwards and forwards
as if tying and then untying a knot.
The man thumps the earth,
the simian leaps up, beyond
the plume of dust beckoned
by the switch's command.
She descends, then vaults
over the whip as it lashes
parallel to the ground.

Raucous cheers and clapping
saturate the air. The monkey scurries
to my feet, bows till she slips
prone in repose. The man spins on his heel,
thumb pressing his forehead.
"Un dullar plezze."
I fumble in my pocket
seeking a threadbare Afghani
to press into his broad hand.
He bows with a flourish, sways back,
as the monkey scurries up his arm,
wobbles on his shoulder.
He hums, content with the take.

Boys' laughter reverberates,
embellishing the eroded mud walls
of compounds narrowing the street.
One by one they relinquish the spell,
scoop up their bundles,
though each hesitates for a moment.

Maestro

Each morning, with proud persistence,
the policeman, perched on a roundabout
scored with black and white stone,
orchestrates the traffic through Kabul.
In his left hand, the baton of stop sign.
His right, circling toward himself,
preempts the polytempo gridlock,
conjectures the drivers' feet
which set in motion the engines' reverberation
in a hierarchy of leadership,
the standard complement
of cars and trucks idling to lurch forward.

Well trained in the nuances of phrasing,
he anticipates the agitation in human nature,
the dynamics for circulation.
His skilled eye carefully notes
the cueing. He leans away.
The intersection responds,
quickly articulates—sharp staccato
gives way to fluid legato.
His palm up, flat, the harmonized vehicles,
an ensemble about to enter
the narrowing of road, halt. Their motors,
in quiet deliberation, a held note.

As It Once Was

In the darkness thunder
rumbles like tanks
full tilt down the hills,
and the night ignites
with gunfire.
Rain through the lamplight,
silvered spray of ballistics,
explodes against the parched earth,
shatters against the window.
The wind advances, then retreats,
falls still.

The drapery of dust that soils
each inch of this city vanishes.
Green turbans of pine sentinels
at corners of walls, within courtyards
vibrate with the ruckus of birds.
Cars and trucks spic and span,
colours revitalized, chrome a high gloss.
Schoolboys swing satchels
as they clamber down streets.
This city remembers,
luxuriates in life as it once was.

Tonight, the city turns back
into itself. People move homeward,
the air raw, woven with dirt,
brown as the rough wool vests
heavy on the shoulders of men.
Women clump the fabric of their burqas,
draw it away from their faces,
shaking the lattice, every few steps,
its fretwork clogged with grime.
Car lights, a tawny yellow, cast
more shadow than beam
through which bicyclists,
heads down, manoeuvre frantically,
scarves rammed into their mouths,
purposeful in their intent
toward shelter, toward home.

Apparition

The cold is insidious, a frigid hand
running along the morning spine.
Fear a heart ailment
beating rapid, erratic.

The land cruiser provides temporary relief
navigating gingerly
over pavement the tanks' ferocity
has disordered, grinding to pebbles.

Still, pock-marked buildings,
as if disease-ravaged,
loiter beyond the thin scars of ice
stretched over open gutter wounds.

The air is choked with smoke.
Residents desperate to stave off invasive chill
stoke their bukhara with whatever
is burnable, close to hand.

Who am I to guess at the pain
or pride of these people?
A fly drawn to the scent of decay
before a hand brushes it away.

Out of the shroud of smoke
a bicyclist apparition.
His legs rise and fall repetitively.
So infectious, the heart takes up his rhythm.

Tethered to his bike, balloons
a whimsy, specters of colour.
They cavort behind him as he passes.
I turn. He vanishes in the opalescent haze.

Zakat

Beyond the roses, which detonate from earth in explosive
crimson, the mosque is illuminated by morning light.

Blue and white tiles incandescent, a flourish of lilies against which
the faithful move—women in white burqas like doves,

men in handwoven shawls encumbering shoulders.
These believers stroll, step out and beyond the shadows

condensed on the ground, dark residue left by gunpowder.
Their lips still flavoured by suhoor, bodies not yet craving

nourishment but braced for cleansing, their hearts
divining purity from worldly activities, inner souls freed

from harm. At one corner, a young boy in a wheelchair,
his legs scarred stumps, extends a hand for zakat.

I conjure the pressure of his soles that day he walked
across a field—perhaps lagging behind playmates

or tending to goats—while from below its surface
the trap sparked forth, entangling him in its fierce release

of metal and energy, shattering him in a split second
of confusion, blood and pain. He smiles at me,

his palm opening, as if in prayer, an aperture for the coins
that now burden my pockets. Exposed to the sunlight

they have the effervescence of fireworks igniting the sky.
As I release them, they are the wings of the birds

the seller in the courtyard has bartered into the hands
of pilgrims. With these offerings we all are released

from the heat and pain of this charred earth,
our voices, like wings, vibrate in the air, repentant with chant.

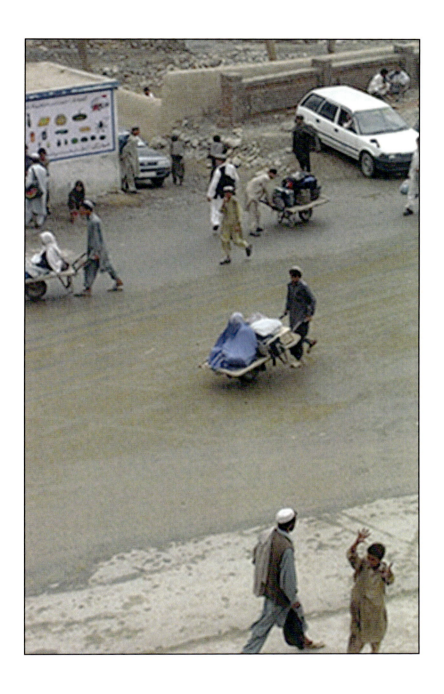

Fragment

Night's cold stiffens the world,
frost blanches everything it touches.
Its rind, splintered by my rubber soles,
articulating silhouettes in the stones
that shift and gnash beneath my weight
as I make my way up to the lookout.

The declining moon, turncoat to its fuller self,
a ghastly face on shattered domes
of palaces where rival forces launched rockets
in a struggle for control. Freedom fighters
rendered dogmatic, edicts murderous as missiles
that commanded the night sky in serpentine fire.

This valley once held a garden resplendent
in flowers and fruits. Now it is reduced,
strewn with tents, like glacier-worn boulders,
in which soldiers sleep, their dreams
a plot of sudden explosions, the havoc of voices
through smoke, women and children crying out.

The sun seizes the horizon, mountain ridges gilded
with promise. Afghans determinedly stir from their beds,
brew tor chai, tear naan to sustain them
past rubble, concrete barriers that reduce
their capital, hold it in a grip, suggest asylum,
a place of refuge, a fragment to hold on to.

Dust

These men's faces give back the somber mountains
rising high above this plain, the punishing winds
gouging deep divides, barren folds and crevices,
the sun's onslaught steeping soil to the pitch of tea.

These men and their families tenacious, scrub brush
wedged between layers of shale, eking out lives
precarious as their goats dangling over edges,
necks craned to tear at limp leaves as they find them.

These elders sitting cross-legged in council, the beaten earth
below them plush with rugs textured by tradition,
designs of their homeland, ever present memories
of what they have fled, of what has been left.

Dervishes of fine powder coat everything.
Mouths and throats are intense with dust. Yet
one man invokes Allah, the guidance of His wisdom,
his voice moist with hope, a spring of water.

The stories that pour forth are of terror and oppression
harder than the rocks among which they scratch,
coaxing what nourishment they can to feed their children,
who stand removed, ravenous for the words of their fathers.

Don't forget us, the camp poet pleads. Listen to the wind.
Its howl is our voice. It has seized our pain and throws it
back at us. We are the dust it scatters here and there,
hurting our eyes like the torture that has scarred our bodies.
.

Acknowledgements

I wish to thank John Buschek, Penn Kemp and Gavin Stairs, whose persistence and confidence inspired me to believe in this collection of poems and photographs and who patiently saw it through to completion. And kudos to Allan Briesmaster, without whose excellent ear and eye this collection would not be as fine as it is. And admiration for the pertinent comments of Pauline Comeau who pushed the poems further.

Much appreciation to Ronnie Brown, Terry Ann Carter, Nadine McInnis, Susan McMaster and Colin Morton, who provided initial comments on some of the earliest drafts of these poems. And thanks to Mary Bramley, Allan and Holly Briesmaster for the assistance with the photo selection.

A great deal of respect and admiration for my colleagues at CIDA, the Canadian Embassy in Kabul, at Foreign Affairs and DND, with whom I worked and traveled to Afghanistan. In particular, thanks to Christopher Alexander, Hau Sing Tse, Doug Williams, Philip Baker, Joe Goodings, Janet Lam, Christian Tardif, Vincent Raiche, Lucie Gauthier, and to Tamim Asey and Nasir Ebrahimkhail in Kabul. Special thanks go to Nipa Banerjee, who was a devoted Head of Aid; Peggy Florida, a kindred spirit; and Pedram Pirnia, a true friend and a gifted photographer, whose image inspired "Marking Time," and who translated the poem "Disheartened Afghans."

And finally, thanks to the City of Ottawa which provided a grant to make work on this book possible.

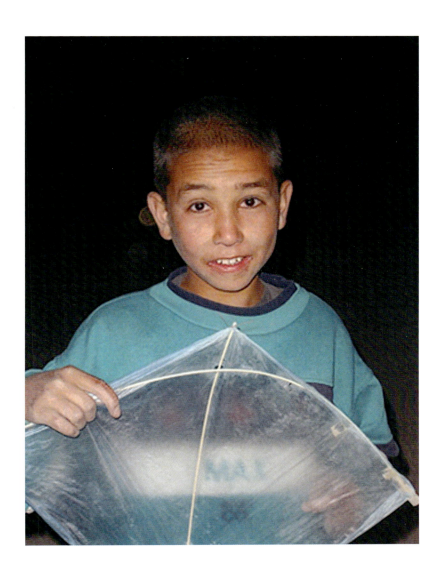